George Melville Baker

Ballads of Bravery

George Melville Baker

Ballads of Bravery

ISBN/EAN: 9783742899637

Manufactured in Europe, USA, Canada, Australia, Japa

Cover: Foto ©Thomas Meinert / pixelio.de

Manufactured and distributed by brebook publishing software (www.brebook.com)

George Melville Baker

Ballads of Bravery

BALLADS OF BRAVERY.

EDITED BY
GEORGE M. BAKER.

WITH

FORTY FULL-PAGE ILLUSTRATIONS.

BOSTON:
LEE AND SHEPARD, PUBLISHERS.
1877.

COPYRIGHT.

LEE AND SHEPARD.

1877.

BOSTON:
ELECTROTYPED BY ALFRED MUDGE AND SON,
SCHOOL STREET.

UNIVERSITY PRESS, CAMBRIDGE:
WELCH, BIGELOW, & CO.

Ballads of Bravery.

Contents.

	PAGE.
"Curfew Must Not Ring To-Night"	13
The Glove and the Lions. — *Leigh Hunt*	18
A Young Hero	21
The Beggar Maid. — *Tennyson*	26
Bunker Hill. — *G. H. Calvert*	29
Fastening the Buckle. — *Samuel Burnham*	34
Hervé Riel. — *Robert Browning*	37
The Battle of Lexington. — *Geo. W. Bungay*	46
The Brave at Home. — *T. Buchanan Read*	50
Kane. — *Fitz James O'Brien*	53
The Life-Boat. — *Alice M. Adams*	58
The Red Jacket. — *George M. Baker*	61

CONTENTS.

Othello's Story of His Life. — *Shakspeare*	66
The Blacksmith of Ragenbach. — *Frank Marry*	70
Marmion and Douglas. — *Scott*	75
The Loss of the Hornet	80
Man the Life-Boat. — *Anon.*	84
Sir Galahad. — *Tennyson*	87
King Canute and His Nobles. — *Dr. Walcott*	92
Outward Bound. — *Anon.*	96
The Brides of Venice. — *Samuel Rogers*	99
The Landing of the Pilgrims. — *Mrs. Hemans*	108
The Days of Chivalry. — *Anon.*	112
The Song of the Camp. — *Anon.*	116
The Recantation of Galileo. — *F. E. Raleigh*	120
Belshazzar. — *Trans. from Heine*	124
Liberty. — From *William Tell*. By *J. Sheridan Knowles*	128
The Fishermen. — *Whittier*	131
Excelsior. — *Longfellow*	137
The Soldier. — *Robert Burns*	140
John Maynard	143
Excalibur. — *Tennyson*	148

CONTENTS.

THE DEATH OF ARTHUR. — *Tennyson*	152
A WET SHEET AND A FLOWING SEA. — *Allan Cunningham*	156
THE LEAP OF CURTIUS. — *Geo. Aspinall*	159
THE RIDE FROM GHENT TO AIX	164
A YARN. — *Mary Howitt*	169

Ballads of Bravery.

"Curfew must not ring To-night"

NGLAND'S sun, bright setting o'er the hills so far away,
  Filled the land with misty beauty at the close of one sad day;
  And the last rays kissed the forehead of a man and maiden fair, —
He with step so slow and weary; she with sunny, floating hair;
He with bowed head, sad and thoughtful; she, with lips so cold and white,
Struggled to keep back the murmur, "Curfew must not ring to-night."

"Sexton," Bessie's white lips faltered, pointing to the prison old,
With its walls so tall and gloomy, walls so dark and damp and cold, —
"I've a lover in that prison, doomed this very night to die
At the ringing of the curfew; and no earthly help is nigh.
Cromwell will not come till sunset," and her face grew strangely white,
As she spoke in husky whispers, "Curfew must not ring to-night."

"Bessie," calmly spoke the sexton (every word pierced her young heart
Like a thousand gleaming arrows, like a deadly poisoned dart),
"Long, long years I've rung the curfew from that gloomy, shadowed tower;
Every evening, just at sunset, it has told the twilight hour.
I have done my duty ever, tried to do it just and right:
Now I'm old, I will not miss it. Girl, the curfew rings to-night!"

Wild her eyes and pale her features, stern and white her thoughtful brow;
And within her heart's deep centre Bessie made a solemn vow.
She had listened while the judges read, without a tear or sigh, —
"At the ringing of the curfew Basil Underwood *must die.*"
And her breath came fast and faster, and her eyes grew large and bright;
One low murmur, scarcely spoken, "Curfew *must not* ring to-night!"

She with light step bounded forward, sprang within the old church-door,
Left the old man coming slowly, paths he 'd trod so oft before.
Not one moment paused the maiden, but, with cheek and brow aglow,
Staggered up the gloomy tower, where the bell swung to and fro;
Then she climbed the slimy ladder, dark, without one ray of light,
Upward still, her pale lips saying, "Curfew *shall not* ring to-night!"

She has reached the topmost ladder; o'er her hangs the great, dark bell,
And the awful gloom beneath her, like the pathway down to hell.
See! the ponderous tongue is swinging; 't is the hour of curfew now,
And the sight has chilled her bosom, stopped her breath, and paled her brow.
Shall she let it ring? No, never! Her eyes flash with sudden light,
As she springs, and grasps it firmly: "Curfew *shall not* ring to-night!"

Out she swung, — far out. The city seemed a tiny speck below, —
There 'twixt heaven and earth suspended, as the bell swung to and fro;
And the half-deaf sexton ringing (years he had not heard the bell),
And he thought the twilight curfew rang young Basil's funeral knell.
Still the maiden, clinging firmly, cheek and brow so pale and white,
Stilled her frightened heart's wild beating: *"Curfew shall not ring to-night!"*

It was o'er, the bell ceased swaying; and the maiden stepped once more
Firmly on the damp old ladder, where, for hundred years before,

Human foot had not been planted; and what she this night had done
Should be told long ages after. As the rays of setting sun
Light the sky with mellow beauty, aged sires, with heads of white,
Tell the children why the curfew did not ring that one sad night.

O'er the distant hills came Cromwell. Bessie saw him; and her brow,
Lately white with sickening horror, glows with sudden beauty now.
At his feet she told her story, showed her hands, all bruised and torn;
And her sweet young face, so haggard, with a look so sad and worn,
Touched his heart with sudden pity, lit his eyes with misty light.
"Go! your lover lives," cried Cromwell. "Curfew shall not ring to-night!"

The Glove and the Lions.

KING FRANCIS was a hearty king and loved a royal sport,
And one day, as his lions fought, sat looking on the court.
The nobles filled the benches, with the ladies in their pride,
And 'mongst them sat the Count de Lorge, with one for whom he sighed.
And truly 't was a gallant thing to see that crowning show, —
Valor and love, and a king above, and the royal beasts below.
Ramped and roared the lions, with horrid laughing jaws;
They bit, they glared, gave blows like beams, a wind went with their paws;
With wallowing might and stifled roar they rolled on one another,
Till all the pit with sand and mane was in a thunderous smother;
The bloody foam above the bars came whizzing through the air.
Said Francis then, "Faith, gentlemen, we're better here than there."

De Lorge's love o'erheard the king, — a beauteous, lively dame,
With smiling lips and sharp bright eyes, which always seemed the same;
She thought, "The count, my lover, is brave as brave can be,
He surely would do wondrous things to show his love of me.
King, ladies, lovers, all look on; the occasion is divine;
I'll drop my glove to prove his love. Great glory will be mine!"
She dropped her glove to prove his love, then looked on him and smiled;
He bowed, and in a moment leaped among the lions wild.
The leap was quick, return was quick, he has regained his place;
Then threw the glove, but not with love, right in the lady's face.
"By Heaven!" said Francis, "rightly done!" rising from where he sat.
"No love," quoth he, "but vanity, sets love a task like that."

A Young Hero.

ON Labrador, like coils of flame
    That clasp the walls of blazing town,
The long, resistless billows came,
    And swept the craggy headlands down;
Till ploughing in strong agonies
    Their furrows deep into the land,
    They carried rocks, and bars of sand
Past farthest margin of old seas,
And in their giant fury bore
Full thirty crowded craft ashore.
That night they pushed the darkness through,
O'er rocks where slippery lichens grew,
And swamps of slime and melted snow,
And torrents filled to overflow,
Through pathless wilds, in showers and wind,
Where woe to him who lags behind!
Where children slipped in ooze, and lay
Half frozen, buried half in clay;
Young mothers, with their babes at breast,
In chilly stupor dropped to rest.

A sailor lad of years fourteen
   Had chanced, as by the waters thrown,
   On four that made sad cry and moan
For parents they had lost between
   The wreck and shore, or haply missed.
   Cheerly and kind their cheeks he kissed,
And folded each in other's arm.
   Upon a sloping mound of moss
   He dragged a heavy sail across,
Close-pinned with bowlders, rough yet warm ;
   And packing it with mosses tight,
   Kept steadfast watch the livelong night,
Nor dared depart, lest e'er again
   Was found this treasure he had hid,
   Some sudden treacherous gust had slid
Beneath that rugged counterpane.
   He knew not name or face of one.
   He saved them. It was nobly done.

Day dawned at last. The storm had lulled;
   And these were happy, sleeping yet.
A few fresh hands of moss he pulled,
Then traced with trembling steps the track
   Of many footprints deeply set;
   And pressing forward, early met
These children's parents hasting back,
   And filled their hearts with boundless joy,
As with blanched lips and chattering teeth
   He told them of his night's employ;
   Feigned, too, he was not much distressed,
Although his dying heart, beneath
   His icy-frozen shirt and vest,

Beat faint. They went; and o'er his eyes
A gathering film beclouded light;
  And music murmured in his brain,
  Such respite sang from toil and strain
That all his senses, wearied quite,
  Were lapped to slumber, lulling pain;
Whilst soothing visions seemed to rise,
  That brought him scenes of other times,
With cherub faces, beaming bright,
  Of many children, and the rhymes
His mother taught him on her knee,
In happy days of infancy.
Then gentlest forms, with rustling wings,
  Were wafting him a world of ease
  Beneath those downy canopies,
Wherewith they shut out angry skies;
And they with winning beckonings —
Who looked so sweet and saintly wise —
His buoyant spirit drew afar
  From creaking timbers, shivering sails,
  And ships that strain in autumn gales,
  And snow-mixed rains, and sleeting hails,
And wind and waves at endless war.
Oh! who will e'er forget the day,
  The bitter tears, the voiceless prayer,
The thoughts of grief we could not say,
The shallow graves within the bay,
  The fifteen dear ones buried there,
The grown, the young, who, side by side,
  Without or coffin, shroud, or priest,
  Were laid; and him we mourned not least, —
The boy that had so bravely died!

The Beggar Maid.

ER arms across her breast she laid;
    She was more fair than words can say;
Barefooted came the beggar maid
    Before the king Cophetua.
In robe and crown the king stept down
    To meet and greet her on her way.
"It is no wonder," said the lords,
    "She is more beautiful than day."

As shines the moon in clouded skies,
    She in her poor attire was seen;
One praised her ankles, one her eyes,
    One her dark hair and lovesome mien.
So sweet a face, such angel grace,
    In all that land had never been·
Cophetua sware a royal oath, —
    "This beggar maid shall be my queen."

Bunker Hill.

"NOT yet, not yet! Steady, steady!"
    On came the foe in even line,
    Nearer and nearer to thrice paces nine.
We looked into their eyes. "Ready!"
A sheet of flame, a roll of death!
They fell by scores: we held our breath.
  Then nearer still they came.
  Another sheet of flame,
And brave men fled who never fled before.
  Immortal fight!
  Foreshadowing flight
Back to the astounded shore.

  Quickly they rallied, re-enforced,
'Mid louder roar of ships' artillery,
And bursting bombs and whistling musketry.
    And shouts and groans anear, afar,
    All the new din of dreadful war.
    Through their broad bosoms calmly coursed
      The blood of those stout farmers, aiming
      For freedom, manhood's birthright claiming.

Onward once more they came.
Another sheet of deathful flame!
 Another and another still!
They broke, they fled,
Again they sped
 Down the green, bloody hill.

Howe, Burgoyne, Clinton, Gage,
Stormed with commanders' rage.
Into each emptied barge
They crowd fresh men for a new charge
Up that great hill.
Again their gallant blood we spill.
That volley was the last:
 Our powder failed.
On three sides fast
 The foe pressed in, nor quailed
A man. Their barrels empty, with musket-stocks
They fought, and gave death-dealing knocks,
Till Prescott ordered the retreat.
Then Warren fell; and through a leaden sleet
From Bunker Hill and Breed,
Stark, Putnam, Pomeroy, Knowlton, Read,
Led off the remnant of those heroes true,
The foe too weakened to pursue.
The ground they gained; but we
 The victory.

The tidings of that chosen band
 Flowed in a wave of power
Over the shaken, anxious land,
 To men, to man, a sudden dower.

History took a fresh, higher start
   From that stanch, beaming hour;
And when the speeding messenger, that bare
The news that strengthened every heart,
Met near the Delaware
The leader, who had just been named,
Who was to be so famed,
   The steadfast, earnest Washington,
With hands uplifted, cries,
His great soul flashing to his eyes,
   "Our liberties are safe! The cause is won!"
A thankful look he cast to heaven, and then
His steed he spurred, in haste to lead such noble men.

Fastening the Buckle.

TAND still, my steed, though the foe is near,
   And sharp the rattle of hoofs on the hill.
And see! there's the glitter of many a spear,
   And a wrathful shout that bodes us ill.
Stand still! Our way is weary and long,
   And muscle and foot are put to the test.
Buckle and girth must be tightened and strong;
   And rider and horse are far from rest.

A moment more, and then we'll skim
   Like a driving cloud o'er hill and plain;
The vision of horseman will slowly dim,
   And pursuer seek the pursued in vain.
Ha! stirrup is strong and girth is tight!
   One bound to the saddle, and off we go.
I count their spears as they glisten bright
   In the ruddy beams of the sunset glow.

'Tis life or death; but we're fresh and strong,
   And buckle and girth are fastened tight.
The race is hard and the way is long,
   But we'll win as twilight fades into night.
Hurrah for rider and horse to-day,
   For buckle and saddle fastened tight!
We'll win! we're gaining! They drop away!
   Our haven of rest is full in sight.

Hervé Riel.

ON the sea and at the Hogue, sixteen hundred ninety-two,
    Did the English fight the French, — woe to France!
And the thirty-first of May, helter-skelter through the blue,
Like a crowd of frightened porpoises a shoal of sharks pursue,
    Came crowding ship on ship to St. Malo on the Rance,
With the English fleet in view.
  'T was the squadron that escaped, with the victor in full chase,
First and foremost of the drove, in his great ship, Damfreville.
    Close on him fled, great and small,
    Twenty-two good ships in all;
    And they signalled to the place,
    "Help the winners of a race!
Get us guidance, give us harbor, take us quick, — or, quicker still,
Here 's the English can and will!"

Then the pilots of the place put out brisk and leaped on board.
"Why, what hope or chance have ships like these to pass?" laughed they.
"Rocks to starboard, rocks to port, all the passage scarred and scored,
Shall the Formidable here, with her twelve and eighty guns,
Think to make the river-mouth by the single narrow way,
Trust to enter where 't is ticklish for a craft of twenty tons,

And with flow at full beside?
Now 't is slackest ebb of tide.
Reach the mooring? Rather say,
While rock stands or water runs,
Not a ship will leave the bay!"

Then was called a council straight;
Brief and bitter the debate:
"Here's the English at our heels; would you have them take in tow
All that's left us of the fleet, linked together stern and bow,
For a prize to Plymouth Sound?
Better run the ships aground!"
(Ended Damfreville his speech.)
"Not a minute more to wait!
Let the captains all and each
Shove ashore, then blow up, burn the vessels on the beach!
France must undergo her fate."

"Give the word!" But no such word
Was ever spoke or heard;
For up stood, for out stepped, for in struck amid all these,
A captain? A lieutenant? A mate, — first, second, third?
No such man of mark, and meet
With his betters to compete,
But a simple Breton sailor, pressed by Tourville for the fleet, —
A poor coasting-pilot he, Hervé Riel, the Croisickese.

And "What mockery or malice have we here?" cries Hervé Riel.
"Are you mad, you Malouins? Are you cowards, fools, or rogues?
Talk to me of rocks and shoals, me who took the soundings, tell
On my fingers every bank, every shallow, every swell
'Twixt the offing here and Grève, where the river disembogues?

Are you bought by English gold? Is it love the lying's for?
    Morn and eve, night and day,
    Have I piloted your bay,
Entered free and anchored fast at the foot of Solidor.
  Burn the fleet, and ruin France? That were worse than fifty Hogues!
Sirs, they know I speak the truth! Sirs, believe me, there's a way!
    Only let me lead the line,
      Have the biggest ship to steer,
      Get this Formidable clear,
    Make the others follow mine,
And I lead them most and least by a passage I know well,
    Right to Solidor, past Greve,
      And there lay them safe and sound ;
      And if one ship misbehave,
      Keel so much as grate the ground, —
Why, I've nothing but my life ; here's my head!" cries Hervé Riel.

    Not a minute more to wait.
    "Steer us in, then, small and great!
Take the helm, lead the line, save the squadron!" cried its chief.
    "Captains, give the sailor place!"
    He is admiral, in brief.
    Still the north-wind, by God's grace.
    See the noble fellow's face
    As the big ship, with a bound,
    Clears the entry like a hound,
Keeps the passage as its inch of way were the wide seas profound!
    See, safe through shoal and rock,
    How they follow in a flock,
Not a ship that misbehaves, not a keel that grates the ground,
    Not a spar that comes to grief!

The peril, see, is past,
  All are harbored to the last;
And just as Hervé Riel halloos, "Anchor!" — sure as fate,
  Up the English come, too late.

So the storm subsides to calm;
  They see the green trees wave
  On the heights o'erlooking Greve.
Hearts that bled are stanched with balm.
"Just our rapture to enhance,
  Let the English rake the bay,
Gnash their teeth and glare askance
  As they cannonade away!
'Neath rampired Solidor pleasant riding on the Rance!"
How hope succeeds despair on each captain's countenance!
Out burst all with one accord,
  "This is Paradise for Hell!
  Let France, let France's king,
  Thank the man that did the thing!"
What a shout, and all one word,
  "Hervé Riel!"
As he stepped in front once more,
  Not a symptom of surprise
  In the frank blue Breton eyes,
Just the same man as before.

Then said Damfreville, "My friend,
I must speak out at the end,
  Though I find the speaking hard:
Praise is deeper than the lips.
You have saved the king his ships,
  You must name your own reward.

Faith, our sun was near eclipse!
Demand whate'er you will,
France remains your debtor still.
Ask to heart's content, and have, or my name's not Damfreville."
Then a beam of fun outbroke
On the bearded mouth that spoke,
As the honest heart laughed through
Those frank eyes of Breton blue:
"Since I needs must say my say,
Since on board the duty's done,
And from Malo Roads to Croisic Point, what is it but a run?
Since 't is ask and have I may,
Since the others go ashore, —
Come, a good whole holiday!
Leave to go and see my wife, whom I call the Belle Aurore!"
That he asked, and that he got, — nothing more.

Name and deed alike are lost;
Not a pillar nor a post
In his Croisic keeps alive the feat as it befell;
Not a head in white and black
On a single fishing-smack
In memory of the man but for whom had gone to rack
All that France saved from the fight whence England bore the bell.
Go to Paris; rank on rank
Search the heroes flung pell-mell
On the Louvre, face and flank,
You shall look long enough ere you come to Hervé Riel.
So, for better and for worse,
Hervé Riel, accept my verse!
In my verse, Hervé Riel, do thou once more
Save the squadron, honor France, love thy wife, the Belle Aurore!

The Battle of Lexington.

THE circling century has brought
   The day on which our fathers fought
   For liberty of deed and thought,
     One hundred years ago!
We crown the day with radiant green,
And buds of hope to bloom between,
And stars undimmed, whose heavenly sheen
    Lights all the world below.

At break of day again we hear
The ringing words of Paul Revere,
And beat of drum and bugle near,
   And shots that shake the throne
Of tyranny, across the sea,
And wake the sons of Liberty
To strike for freedom and be free:—
    Our king is God alone!

"Load well with powder and with ball,
Stand firmly, like a living wall;
But fire not till the foe shall call
    A shot from every one,"

Said Parker to his gallant men.
Then Pitcairn dashed across the plain,
Discharged an angry threat, and then
    The world heard Lexington!

Militia and brave minute-men
Stood side by side upon the plain,
Unsheltered in the storm of rain,
    Of fire, and leaden sleet;
But through the gray smoke and the flame,
Star crowned, a white-winged angel came,
To bear aloft the souls of flame
    From war's red winding-sheet!

Hancock and Adams glory won
With yeomen whose best work was done
At Concord and at Lexington,
    When first they struck the blow.
Long may their children's children bear
Upon wide shoulders, fit to wear,
The mantles that fell through the air
    One hundred years ago!

The Brave at Home.

THE maid who binds her warrior's sash,
    With smile that well her pain dissembles,
  The while beneath her drooping lash
    One starry tear-drop hangs and trembles,
Though heaven alone records the tear,
  And fame shall never know the story,
Her heart has shed a drop as dear
  As e'er bedewed the field of glory.

The wife who girds her husband's sword,
  'Mid little ones who weep or wonder,
And bravely speaks the cheering word,
  What though her heart be rent asunder,
Doomed nightly in her dreams to hear
  The bolts of death around him rattle,
Hath shed as sacred blood as e'er
  Was poured upon a field of battle!

The mother who conceals her grief,
  While to her breast her son she presses,
Then breathes a few brave words and brief,
  Kissing the patriot brow she blesses,
With no one but her secret God
  To know the pain that weighs upon her,
Sheds holy blood as e'er the sod
  Received on Freedom's field of honor!

Kane: died February 16, 1857.

LOFT upon an old basaltic crag,
    Which, scalped by keen winds that defend the Pole,
    Gazes with dead face on the seas that roll
    Around the secret of the mystic zone,
A mighty nation's star-bespangled flag
        Flutters alone;
And underneath, upon the lifeless front
    Of that drear cliff, a simple name is traced, —
Fit type of him who, famishing and gaunt,
    But with a rocky purpose in his soul,
        Breasted the gathering snows,
        Clung to the drifting floes,
By want beleaguered and by winter chased,
Seeking the brother lost amid that frozen waste.

Not many months ago we greeted him,
    Crowned with the icy honors of the North.
    Across the land his hard-won fame went forth,
And Maine's deep woods were shaken limb by limb;
His own mild Keystone State, sedate and prim,
    Burst from decorous quiet as he came;
    Hot Southern lips, with eloquence aflame,
Sounded his triumph; Texas, wild and grim,

Proffered its horny hand; the large-lunged West,
    From out his giant breast,
Yelled its frank welcome; and from main to main,
        Jubilant to the sky,
        Thundered the mighty cry,
          HONOR TO KANE!

  .   .   .   .   .   .

He needs no tears, who lived a noble life!
  We will not weep for him who died so well,
  But we will gather round the hearth and tell
      The story of his strife.
      Such homage suits him well, —
  Better than funeral pomp or passing bell.

What tale of peril and self-sacrifice,
Prisoned amid the fastnesses of ice,
With hunger howling o'er the wastes of snow;
Night lengthening into months; the ravenous floe
Crunching the massive ships, as the white bear
Crunches his prey. The insufficient share
        Of loathsome food;
The lethargy of famine; the despair
  Uurging to labor, nervelessly pursued;
  Toil done with skinny arms, and faces hued
Like pallid masks, while dolefully behind
Glimmered the fading embers of a mind!

That awful hour, when through the prostrate band
Delirium stalked, laying his burning hand
Upon the ghastly foreheads of the crew;
The whispers of rebellion, faint and few

At first, but deepening ever till they grew
Into black thoughts of murder: such the throng
Of horrors bound the hero. High the song
Should be that hymns the noble part he played!
Sinking himself, yet ministering aid
To all around him. By a mighty will
Living defiant of the wants that kill,
  Because his death would seal his comrades' fate;
Cheering, with ceaseless and inventive skill,
  Those Polar waters, dark and desolate.
  Equal to every trial, every fate,
He stands, until spring, tardy with relief,
    Unlocks the icy gate,
And the pale prisoners thread the world once more,
To the steep cliffs of Greenland's pastoral shore,
    Bearing their dying chief.

Time was when he should gain his spurs of gold
  From royal hands, who wooed the knightly state.
The knell of old formalities is tolled,
  And the world's knights are now self-consecrate.
No grander episode doth chivalry hold
  In all its annals, back to Charlemagne,
  Than that lone vigil of unceasing pain,
Faithfully kept through hunger and through cold,
  By the good Christian knight, Elisha Kane!

The Life-Boat.

LAUNCH the life-boat! Far on high
    The fiery rockets gleam,
While loud and clear the booming signal gun
Says there is work that quickly must be done.
A vessel's in distress: haste, every one,
    Nor idly stop to dream.

Launch the life-boat! On the shore
    The startled people stand,
And watch the signal lights that shine on high,
And through the pitchy darkness seek to spy
The struggling ship, or to their comrades try
    To lend a helping hand.

Launch the life-boat! Now the moon
    Sheds forth her silvery light,
And shows the boat is off; one long, loud cheer
Breaks from the eager crowd assembled here;
The dip of oars comes to the listening ear,
    Upon the silent night.

Speed the life-boat and her crew,
    Speed them on their watery way!
As joy and hope they bring to hearts cast down,
And waiting 'neath the storm-clouds' dismal frown,
While wind and wave their trembling voices drown,
    Waiting another day.

THE RED JACKET.

'TIS a cold, bleak night. With angry roar
    The north winds beat and clamor at the door;
    The drifted snow lies heaped along the street,
    Swept by a blinding storm of hail and sleet;
The clouded heavens no guiding starlight lend,
But o'er the earth in gloom and darkness bend;
Gigantic shadows, by the night-lamps thrown,
Dance their weird revels fitfully alone.

In lofty halls, where fortune takes its ease,
Sunk in the treasures of all lands and seas;
In happy homes, where warmth and comfort meet
The weary traveller with their smiles to greet;
In lonely dwellings, where the needy swarm
Round starving embers, chilling limbs to warm,—
Rises the prayer that makes the sad heart light,
"Thank God for home this bitter, bitter night!"

But hark! above the beating of the storm
Peals on the startled ear the fire-alarm!
Yon gloomy heaven's aflame with sudden light;
And heart-beats quicken with a strange affright.
From tranquil slumber springs, at duty's call,
The ready friend no danger can appall;
Fierce for the conflict, sturdy, true, and brave,
He hurries forth to battle and to save.

From yonder dwelling fiercely shooting out,
Devouring all they coil themselves about,
The flaming furies, mounting high and higher,
Wrap the frail structure in a cloak of fire.
Strong arms are battling with the stubborn foe,
In vain attempts their power to overthrow;
With mocking glee they revel with their prey,
Defying human skill to check their way.

And see! far up above the flames' hot breath,
Something that's human waits a horrid death:
A little child, with waving golden hair,
Stands like a phantom 'mid the horrid glare,
Her pale, sweet face against the window pressed,
While sobs of terror shake her tender breast.
And from the crowd beneath, in accents wild,
A mother screams, "O God! my child, my child!"

Up goes a ladder! Through the startled throng
A hardy fireman swiftly moves along,
Mounts sure and fast along the slender way,
Fearing no danger, dreading but delay.
The stifling smoke-clouds lower in his path,
Sharp tongues of flame assail him in their wrath;
But up, still up he goes! The goal is won,
His strong arm beats the sash, and he is gone,—

Gone to his death. The wily flames surround,
And burn and beat his ladder to the ground;
In flaming columns move with quickened beat,
To rear a massive wall 'gainst his retreat.

Courageous heart, thy mission was so pure,
Suffering humanity must thy loss deplore:
Henceforth with martyred heroes thou shalt live,
Crowned with all honors nobleness can give.

Nay, not so fast! subdue these gloomy fears!
Behold! he quickly on the roof appears,
Bearing the tender child, his jacket warm
Flung round her shrinking form to guard from harm.
Up with your ladders! Quick! 't is but a chance!
Behold how fast the roaring flames advance!
Quick! quick! brave spirits to his rescue fly!
Up! up! by heavens, this hero must not die!

Silence! he comes along the burning road,
Bearing with tender care his living load.
Aha! he totters! Heaven in mercy save
The good, true heart that can so nobly brave!
He 's up again, and now he 's coming fast!
One moment, and the fiery ordeal 's past,
And now he 's safe! Bold flames, ye fought in vain!
A happy mother clasps her child again.

"O, Heaven bless you!" 'T is an earnest prayer
Which grateful thousands with that mother share.
Heaven bless the brave who on the war-clad field
Stand fast, stand firm, the nation's trusty shield!
Heaven bless the brave who on the mighty sea
Fearless uphold the standard of the free!
And Heaven's choicest blessing for the brave
Who fearless move our lives and homes to save!

OTHELLO'S STORY OF HIS LIFE.

HER father loved me; oft invited me;
Still questioned me the story of my life
From year to year; the battles, sieges, fortunes,
   That I had past.
I ran it through, e'en from my boyish days,
To the very moment that he bade me tell it.
Wherein I spake of most disastrous chances,
Of moving accidents by flood and field,
Of hair-breadth 'scapes, in the imminent deadly breach,
Of being taken by the insolent foe,
And sold to slavery; of my redemption thence,
And with it all my travel's history.
. . . .
                              All these to hear,
Would Desdemona seriously incline;
But still the house affairs would draw her thence,
Whichever as she could with haste despatch,
She'd come again, and with a greedy ear
Devour up my discourse. Which, I observing,
Took once a pliant hour, and found good means
To draw from her a prayer of earnest heart
That I would all my pilgrimage dilate,
Whereof, by parcels, she had something heard,
But not distinctly.

                                             I did consent;
And often did beguile her of her tears,
When I did speak of some distressful stroke
That my youth suffered. My story being done,
She gave me for my pains a world of sighs.
She swore in faith, 't was strange, 't was passing strange;
'T was pitiful, 't was wondrous pitiful;
She wished she had not heard it; yet she wished
That heaven had made her such a man.
                                             She thanked me,
And bade me, if I had a friend that loved her,
I should but teach him how to tell my story,
And that would woo her. On this hint I spake;
She loved me for the dangers I had passed;
And I loved her that she did pity them:
This is the only witchcraft which I 've used.

The Blacksmith of Ragenbach.

In a little German village,
  On the waters of the Rhine,
Gay and joyous in their pastimes,
  In the pleasant vintage-time,
Were a group of happy peasants,
  For the day released from toil,
Thanking God for all his goodness
  In the product of their soil,

When a cry rung through the welkin,
  And appeared upon the scene
A panting dog, with crest erect,
  Foaming mouth, and savage mien.
"He is mad!" was shrieked in chorus.
  In dismay they all fell back, —
All, except one towering figure, —
  'Twas the smith of Ragenbach.

God had given this man his image;
  Nature stamped him as complete.
Now it was incumbent on him
  To perform a greater feat
Than Horatius at the bridge,
  When he stood on Tiber's bank;
For behind him were his townsfolk,
  Who, appalled with terror, shrank

From the most appalling danger, —
    That which makes the bravest quail, —
While they all were grouped together,
    Shaking limbs and visage pale.
For a moment cowered the beast,
    Snapping to the left and right,
While the blacksmith stood before him
    In the power of his might.

"*One* must die to save the many,
    Let it then my duty be;
I've the power. Fear not, neighbors!
    From this peril you'll be free."
As the lightning from the storm-cloud
    Leaps to earth with sudden crash,
So upon the rabid monster
    Did this man and hero dash.

In the death-grip then they struggled,
    Man and dog, with scarce a sound,
Till from out the fearful conflict
    Rose the man from off the ground,
Gashed and gory from the struggle;
    But the beast lay stiff and dead.
There he stood, while people gathered,
    And rained blessings on his head.

"Friends," he said, "from one great peril,
    With God's help, I've set you free,
But my task is not yet ended,
    There is danger now in *me*.

"Yet secure from harm you shall be,
  None need fear before I die.
That my sufferings may be shortened,
  Ask of Him who rules on high."

Then unto his forge he straightway
  Walked erect, with rapid step,
While the people followed after,
  Some with shouts, while others wept;
And with nerve as steady as when
  He had plied his trade for gain,
He selected, without faltering,
  From his store, the heaviest chain.

To his anvil first he bound it,
  Next his limb he shackled fast,
Then he said unto his townsfolk,
  "All your danger now is past.
Place within my reach, I pray you,
  Food and water for a time,
Until God shall ease my sufferings
  By his gracious will divine."

Long he suffered, but at last
  Came a summons from on high,
Then his soul, with angel escort,
  Sought its home beyond the sky;
And the people of that village,
  Those whom he had died to save,
Still with grateful hearts assemble,
  And with flowers bedeck his grave.

Marmion and Douglas.

Not far advanced was morning day,
   When Marmion did his troop array
      To Surrey's camp to ride.
He had safe-conduct for his band,
Beneath the royal seal and hand,
   And Douglas gave a guide.
The ancient earl, with stately grace,
Would Clara on her palfrey place,
And whispered in an undertone,
"Let the hawk stoop, his prey is flown."
The train from out the castle drew,
But Marmion stopped to bid adieu:
   "Though something I might 'plain," he said,
   "Of cold respect to stranger guest,
Sent hither by your king's behest,
   While in Tantallon's towers I stayed,
Part we in friendship from your land,
And, noble earl, receive my hand."
But Douglas round him drew his cloak,
Folded his arms, and thus he spoke:
"My manors, halls, and bowers shall still
Be open, at my sovereign's will,
To each one whom he lists, howe'er
Unmeet to be the owner's peer;

My castles are my king's alone,
From turret to foundation-stone,—
The hand of Douglas is his own,
And never shall in friendly grasp
The hand of such as Marmion clasp."

Burned Marmion's swarthy cheek like fire,
And shook his very frame for ire,
  And—"This to me!" he said;—
"An' twere not for thy hoary beard,
Such hand as Marmion's had not spared
To cleave the Douglas' head!
And first, I tell thee, haughty peer,
He who does England's message here,
Although the meanest in her state,
May well, proud Angus, be thy mate!
And Douglas, more, I tell thee here,
Even in thy pitch of pride,
Here in thy hold, thy vassals near,
(Nay, never look upon your lord,
And lay your hands upon your sword,)
  I tell thee, thou 'rt defied!
And if thou saidst I am not peer
To any lord in Scotland here,
Lowland or Highland, far or near,
  Lord Angus, thou hast lied!"
On the earl's cheek the flush of rage
O'ercame the ashen hue of age;
Fierce he broke forth, "And dar'st thou then
To beard the lion in his den,
  The Douglas in his hall?

And hop'st thou hence unscathed to go?
No, by St. Bride of Bothwell, no!
Up drawbridge, grooms! What, warder, ho!
  Let the portcullis fall."
Lord Marmion turned,—well was his need!—
And dashed the rowels in his steed,
Like arrow through the archway sprung;
The ponderous grate behind him rung:
To pass there was such scanty room,
The bars, descending, razed his plume.

The steed along the drawbridge flies,
Just as it trembled on the rise;
Not lighter does the swallow skim
Along the smooth lake's level brim;
And when Lord Marmion reached his band,
He halts, and turns with clinched hand,
And shout of loud defiance pours,
And shook his gauntlet at the towers.
"Horse! horse!" the Douglas cried, "and chase!"
But soon he reigned his fury's pace:
"A royal messenger he came,
Though most unworthy of the name.

. . . . . .

St. Mary mend my fiery mood!
Old age ne'er cools the Douglas blood,
I thought to slay him where he stood.
'T is pity of him, too," he cried;
"Bold can he speak and fairly ride,
I warrant him a warrior tried."
With this his mandate he recalls,
And slowly seeks his castle walls.

The Loss of the Hornet.

CALL the watch! call the watch!
   "Ho! the starboard watch, ahoy!" Have you heard
   How a noble ship so trim, like our own, my hearties, here,
All scudding 'fore the gale, disappeared,
   Where yon southern billows roll o'er their bed so green and clear?
Hold the reel! keep her full! hold the reel!
   How she flew athwart the spray, as, shipmates, we do now,
Till her twice a hundred fearless hearts of steel
   Felt the whirlwind lift its waters aft, and plunge her downward bow!
      Bear a hand!

Strike top-gallants! mind your helm! jump aloft!
   'T was such a night as this, my lads, a rakish bark was drowned,
When demons foul, that whisper seamen oft,
   Scooped a tomb amid the flashing surge that never shall be found.
Square the yards! a double reef! Hark the blast!
   O, fiercely has it fallen on the war-ship of the brave,
When its tempest fury stretched the stately mast
   All along her foamy sides, as they shouted on the wave,
      "Bear a hand!"

Call the watch! call the watch!
   "Ho! the larboard watch, ahoy!" Have you heard
   How a vessel, gay and taut, on the mountains of the sea,
Went below, with all her warlike crew on board,

They who battled for the happy, boys, and perished for the free?
    Clew, clew up, fore and aft! keep away!
How the vulture bird of death, in its black and viewless form,
    Hovered sure o'er the clamors of his prey,
While through all their dripping shrouds yelled the spirit of the storm!
        Bear a hand!

Now out reefs! brace the yards! lively there!
    O, no more to homeward breeze shall her swelling bosom spread,
But love's expectant eye bid despair
    Set her raven watch eternal o'er the wreck in ocean's bed.
Board your tacks! cheerly, boys! But for them,
    Their last evening gun is fired, their gales are overblown;
O'er their smoking deck no starry flag shall stream;
    They'll sail no more, they'll fight no more, for their gallant ship's gone down.
        Bear a hand!

Man the Life-Boat.

Man the life-boat! Man the life-boat!
  Help, or yon ship is lost!
Man the life-boat! Man the life-boat!
  See how she's tempest-tossed.
No human power in such an hour
  The gallant bark can save;
Her mainmast gone, and running on,
  She seeks her watery grave.
Man the life-boat! Man the life-boat!
  See, the dreaded signal flies!
Ha! she's struck, and from the wreck
  Despairing shouts arise.

O, speed the life-boat! Speed the life-boat!
  O God, their efforts crown!
She dashes on; the ship is gone,
  Full forty fathoms down.
And see, the crew are struggling now
  Amidst the tempest roar.
They're in the boat, they're all afloat, —
  Hurrah! they've gained the shore.
Bless the life-boat! Bless the life-boat!
  O God, thou'lt hear our prayer!
Bless the life-boat! Bless the life-boat!
  No longer we'll despair.

SIR GALAHAD.

My good blade carves the casques of men,
  My tough lance thrusteth sure,
My strength is as the strength of ten,
  Because my heart is pure.
The shattering trumpet shrilleth high,
  The hard brands shiver on the steel,
The splintered spear-shafts crack and fly,
  The horse and rider reel:
They reel, they roll in clanging lists,
  And when the tide of combat stands,
Perfume and flowers fall in showers,
  That lightly rain from ladies' hands.

How sweet are looks that ladies bend
  On whom their favors fall!
For them I battle till the end,
  To save from shame and thrall:
But all my heart is drawn above,
  My knees are bowed in crypt and shrine:
I never felt the kiss of love,
  Nor maiden's hand in mine.
More bounteous aspects on me beam,
  Me mightier transports move and thrill;
So keep I fair through faith and prayer
  A virgin heart in work and will.

When down the stormy crescent goes,
  A light before me swims,
Between dark stems the forest glows,
  I hear a noise of hymns:
Then by some secret shrine I ride;
  I hear a voice, but none are there;
The stalls are void, the doors are wide,
  The tapers burning fair.
Fair gleams the snowy altar-cloth,
  The silver vessels sparkle clean,
The shrill bell rings, the censer swings,
  And solemn chants resound between.

Sometimes on lonely mountain-meres
  I find a magic bark;
I leap on board: no helmsman steers:
  I float till all is dark.
A gentle sound, an awful light!
  Three angels bear the holy Grail:
With folded feet, in stoles of white,
  On sleeping wings they sail.
Ah, blessed vision! blood of God!
  My spirit beats her mortal bars,
As down dark tides the glory slides,
  And star-like mingles with the stars.

When on my goodly charger borne
  Through dreaming towns I go,
The cock crows ere the Christmas morn,
  The streets are dumb with snow.
The tempest crackles on the leads,
  And, ringing, springs from brand and mail;

But o'er the dark a glory spreads,
   And gilds the driving hail.
I leave the plain, I climb the height;
   No branchy thicket shelter yields;
But blessed forms in whistling storms
   Fly o'er waste fens and windy fields.

A maiden knight, to me is given
   Such hope, I know not fear;
I yearn to breathe the airs of heaven
   That often meet me here.
I muse on joy that will not cease,
   Pure spaces clothed in living beams,
Pure lilies of eternal peace,
   Whose odors haunt my dreams;
And, stricken by an angel's hand,
   This mortal armor that I wear,
This weight and size, this heart and eyes,
   Are touched, are turned to finest air.

The clouds are broken in the sky,
   And through the mountain-walls
A rolling organ-harmony
   Swells up, and shakes and falls.
Then move the trees, the copses nod,
   Wings flutter, voices hover clear:
"O just and faithful knight of God,
   Ride on! the prize is near."
So pass I hostel, hall, and grange;
   By bridge and ford, by park and pale,
All armed I ride, whate'er betide,
   Until I find the holy Grail.

King Canute and his Nobles

Canute was by his nobles taught to fancy
    That, by a kind of royal necromancy,
        He had the power old Ocean to control.
Down rushed the royal Dane upon the strand,
    And issued, like a Solomon, command, — poor soul!

"Go back, ye waves, you blustering rogues," quoth he;
"Touch not your lord and master, Sea;
    For by my power almighty, if you do — "
Then, staring vengeance, out he held a stick,
Vowing to drive old Ocean to Old Nick,
    Should he even wet the latchet of his shoe.

The sea retired, — the monarch fierce rushed on,
    And looked as if he'd drive him from the land;
But Sea, not caring to be put upon,
    Made for a moment a bold stand.

Not only made a stand did Mr. Ocean,
But to his waves he made a motion,
    And bid them give the king a hearty trimming.
The order seemed a deal the waves to tickle,
For soon they put his Majesty in pickle,
    And set his royalties, like geese, a swimming.

All hands aloft, with one tremendous roar,
Sound did they make him wish himself on shore;
   His head and ears they most handsomely doused, —
Just like a porpoise, with one general shout,
The waves so tumbled the poor king about.
   No anabaptist e'er was half so soused.

At length to land he crawled, a half-drowned thing,
Indeed, more like a crab than like a king,
   And found his courtiers making rueful faces;
But what said Canute to the lords and gentry,
Who hailed him from the water, on his entry,
   All trembling for their lives or places?

"My lords and gentlemen, by your advice,
   I've had with Mr. Sea a pretty bustle;
My treatment from my foe, not overnice,
   Just made a jest for every shrimp and mussel.

"A pretty trick for one of my dominion!
My lords, I thank you for your great opinion.
You'll tell me, p'r'aps, I've only lost one game
   And bid me try another, — for the rubber.
Permit me to inform you all, with shame,
   That you're a set of knaves and I'm a lubber."

OUTWARD BOUND.

CLINK — clink — clink! goes our windlass.
    "Ahoy!" "Haul in!" "Let go!"
  Yards braced and sails set,
    Flags uncurl and flow.
Some eyes that watch from shore are wet,
  (How bright their welcome shone!)
While, bending softly to the breeze,
And rushing through the parted seas,
  Our gallant ship glides on.
Though one has left a sweetheart,
  And one has left a wife,
'T will never do to mope and fret,
  Or curse a sailor's life.
See, far away they signal yet, —
  They dwindle — fade — they're gone:
For, dashing outwards, bold and brave,
And springing light from wave to wave,
  Our merry ship flies on.
Gay spreads the sparkling ocean;
  But many a gloomy night
And stormy morrow must be met
  Ere next we heave in sight.
The parting look we'll ne'er forget,
  The kiss, the benison,
As round the rolling world we go.
God bless you all! Blow, breezes blow!
  Sail on, good ship, sail on!

The Brides of Venice.

'T was St. Mary's eve; and all poured forth,
  As to some grand solemnity. The fisher
  Came from his islet, bringing o'er the waves
His wife and little one; the husbandman
From the Firm Land, along the Po, the Brenta,
Crowding the common ferry. All arrived;
And in his straw the prisoner turned and listened,
So great the stir in Venice. Old and young
Thronged her three hundred bridges; the grave Turk,
Turbaned, long-vested, and the cozening Jew,
In yellow hat and threadbare gabardine,
Hurrying along. For, as the custom was,
The noblest sons and daughters of the state,
They of patrician birth, the flower of Venice,
Whose names are written in the "Book of Gold,"
Were on that day to solemnize their nuptials.

  At noon, a distant murmur through the crowd,
Rising and rolling on, announced their coming;
And never from the first was to be seen
Such splendor or such beauty. Two and two
(The richest tapestry unrolled before them),
First came the brides in all their loveliness;
Each in her veil, and by two bridesmaids followed,

Only less lovely, who behind her bore
The precious caskets that within contained
The dowry and the presents. On she moved,
Her eyes cast down, and holding in her hand
A fan, that gently waved, of ostrich feathers.
Her veil, transparent as the gossamer,
Fell from beneath a starry diadem;
And on her dazzling neck a jewel shone,
Ruby or diamond or dark amethyst:
A jewelled chain, in many a winding wreath,
Wreathing her gold brocade.
       Before the church,
That venerable pile on the sea-brink,
Another train they met, — no strangers to them, —
Brothers to some, and to the rest still dearer,
Each in his hand bearing his cap and plume,
And, as he walked, with modest dignity
Folding his scarlet mantle, his *Jabarro*.

 They join, they enter in, and up the aisle
Led by the full-voiced choir, in bright procession,
Range round the altar. In his vestments there
The patriarch stands; and while the anthem flows,
Who can look on unmoved? Mothers in secret
Rejoicing in the beauty of their daughters;
Sons in the thought of making them their own;
And they, arrayed in youth and innocence,
Their beauty heightened by their hopes and fears

 At length the rite is ending. All fall down
In earnest prayer, all of all ranks together;
And stretching out his hands, the holy man
Proceeds to give the general benediction,
When hark! a din of voices from without,

And shrieks and groans and outcries, as in battle;
And lo! the door is burst, the curtain rent,
And armed ruffians, robbers from the deep,
Savage, uncouth, led on by Barbarigo
And his six brothers in their coats of steel,
Are standing on the threshold! Statue-like,
Awhile they gaze on the fallen multitude,
Each with his sabre up, in act to strike;
Then, as at once recovering from the spell,
Rush forward to the altar, and as soon
Are gone again, amid no clash of arms,
Bearing away the maidens and the treasures.

 Where are they now? Ploughing the distant waves,
Their sails all set, and they upon the deck
Standing triumphant. To the east they go,
Steering for Istria, their accursed barks
(Well are they known, the galliot and the galley)
Freighted with all that gives to life its value
The richest argosies were poor to them!

 Now might you see the matrons running wild
Along the beach; the men half armed and arming;
One with a shield, one with a casque and spear;
One with an axe, hewing the mooring-chain
Of some old pinnace. Not a raft, a plank,
But on that day was drifting. In an hour
Half Venice was afloat. But long before,—
Frantic with grief, and scorning all control,—
The youths were gone in a light brigantine,
Lying at anchor near the arsenal;
Each having sworn, and by the holy rood,
To slay or to be slain.
     And from the tower

The watchman gives the signal. In the east
A ship is seen, and making for the port;
Her flag St. Mark's. And now she turns the point,
Over the waters like a sea-bird flying.
Ha! 't is the same, 't is theirs! From stern to prow
Hung with green boughs, she comes, she comes, restoring
All that was lost!
     Coasting, with narrow search,
Friuli, like a tiger in his spring,
They had surprised the corsairs where they lay,
Sharing the spoil in blind security,
And casting lots; had slain them one and all, —
All to the last, — and flung them far and wide
Into the sea, their proper element.
Him first, as first in rank, whose name so long
Had hushed the babes of Venice, and who yet
Breathing a little, in his look retained
The fierceness of his soul.
     Thus were the brides
Lost and recovered. And what now remained
But to give thanks? Twelve breastplates and twelve crowns,
Flaming with gems and gold, the votive offerings
Of the young victors to their patron saint,
Vowed on the field of battle, were erelong
Laid at his feet; and to preserve forever
The memory of a day so full of change,
From joy to grief, from grief to joy again,
Through many an age, as oft as it came round,
'T was held religiously with all observance.
The Doge resigned his crimson for pure ermine;
And through the city in a stately barge
Of gold were borne, with songs and symphonies,

Twelve ladies young and noble. Clad they were
In bridal white with bridal ornaments,
Each in her glittering veil; and on the deck
As on a burnished throne, they glided by.
No window or balcony but adorned
With hangings of rich texture; not a roof
But covered with beholders, and the air
Vocal with joy. Onward they went, their oars
Moving in concert with the harmony,
Through the Rialto to the ducal palace;
And at a banquet there, served with due honor,
Sat, representing in the eyes of all —
Eyes not unwet, I ween, with grateful tears —
Their lovely ancestors, the "Brides of Venice."

The Landing of the Pilgrim Fathers.

THE breaking waves dashed high
  On a stern and rock-bound coast,
And the woods against a stormy sky
  Their giant branches tossed;

And the heavy night hung dark
  The hills and water o'er,
When a band of exiles moored their bark
  On the wild New England shore.

Not as the conqueror comes,
  They, the true-hearted, came;
Not with the roll of the stirring drums,
  And the trumpet that sings of fame;

Not as the flying come,
  In silence and in fear;
They shook the depths of the desert gloom
  With their hymns of lofty cheer.

Amidst the storm they sang,
  And the stars heard, and the sea;
And the sounding aisles of the dim woods rang
  To the anthem of the free!

The ocean eagle soared
  From his nest by the white wave's foam,
And the rocking pines of the forest roared,—
  This was their welcome home.

There were men with hoary hair
  Amidst that pilgrim band:
Why had they come to wither there,
  Away from their childhood's land?

There was woman's fearless eye,
  Lit by her deep love's truth;
There was manhood's brow, serenely high,
  And the fiery heart of youth.

What sought they thus afar?
  Bright jewels of the mine,
The wealth of seas, the spoils of war?
  They sought a faith's pure shrine!

Aye, call it holy ground,
  The soil where first they trod;
They have left unstained what there they found,—
  Freedom to worship God.

The Days of Chivalry.

ALAS! the days of chivalry are fled,
    The brilliant tournament exists no more;
Our loves are cold, and dull as ice or lead,
    And courting is a most enormous bore.

In those good "olden times," a "ladye bright"
    Might sit within her turret or her bower,
While lovers sang and played without all night,
    And deemed themselves rewarded by a flower.

Yet if one favored swain would persevere,
    In despite of her haughty scorn and laugh,
Perchance she threw him, with the closing year,
    An old odd glove, or else a worn-out scarf.

Off then, away he'd ride o'er sea and land,
    And dragons fell and mighty giants smite
With the tough spear he carried in his hand;
    And all to prove himself her own true knight.

Meanwhile a thousand more, as wild as he,
  Were all employed upon the self-same thing ;
And when each had rode hard for his "ladye,"
  They all come back and met within a ring.

Where all the men who were entitled "syr"
  Appeared with martial air and haughty frown,
Bearing "long poles, each other up to stir,"
  And, in the stir-up, thrust each other down.

And then they galloped round with dire intent,
  Each knight resolved another's pride to humble ;
And laughter rang around the tournament
  As oft as any of them had a tumble.

And when, perchance, some ill-starred wight might die,
  The victim of a stout, unlucky poke,
Mayhap some fair one wiped one beauteous eye,
  The rest smiled calmly on the deadly joke.

Soon, then, the lady, whose grim, stalwart swain
  Had got the strongest horse and toughest pole,
Bedecked him, kneeling, with a golden chain,
  And plighted troth before the motley whole.

Alas! the days of chivalry are fled,
  The brilliant tournament exists no more,
Men now are cold and dull as ice or lead,
  And even courtship is a dreadful bore.

The Song of the Camp.

"Give us a song!" the soldiers cried,
   The outer trenches guarding,
When the heated guns of the camps allied
   Grew weary of bombarding.

The dark Redan, in silent scoff,
   Lay grim and threatening under;
And the tawny mound of the Malakoff
   No longer belched its thunder.

There was a pause. A guardsman said,
   "We storm the forts to-morrow;
Sing while we may, another day
   Will bring enough of sorrow."

They lay along the battery's side,
   Below the smoking cannon,
Brave hearts from Severn and from Clyde,
   And from the banks of Shannon.

They sang of love, and not of fame;
   Forgot was Britain's glory:
Each heart recalled a different name,
   But all sang "Annie Lawrie."

Voice after voice caught up the song,
   Until its tender passion
Rose like an anthem, rich and strong,—
   Their battle-eve confession.

Beyond the darkening ocean burned
   The bloody sunset's embers,
While the Crimean valleys learned
   How English love remembers.

And once again a fire of hell
   Rained on the Russian quarters,
With scream of shot and burst of shell
   And bellowing of the mortars!

And Irish Nora's eyes are dim
   For a singer dumb and gory;
And English Mary mourns for him
   Who sang of "Annie Lawrie."

Sleep, soldiers! still in honored rest
   Your truth and valor wearing,
The bravest are the tenderest,
   The loving are the daring.

The Recantation of Galileo.

FAR 'neath the glorious light of the noontide,
  In a damp dungeon a prisoner lay,
Aged and feeble, his failing years numbered,
  Waiting the fate to be brought him that day.

Silence, oppressive with darkness, held durance;
  Death in the living, or living in death;
Crouched on the granite, and burdened with fetters,
  Inhaling slow poison with each labored breath.

O'er the damp floor of his dungeon there glistened
  Faintly the rays of a swift-nearing light;
Then the sweet jingle of keys, that soon opened
  The door, and revealed a strange scene to his sight.

In the red glare of the flickering torches,
  Held by the gray-gownèd soldiers of God,
Gathered a group that the world will remember
  Long ages after we sleep 'neath the sod.

Draped in their robes of bright scarlet and purple,
  Bearing aloft the gold emblems of Rome,
Stood the chief priests of the papal dominion,
  Under the shadow of Peter's proud dome,

By the infallible pontiff commanded,
    From his own lips their directions received;
Sent to demand of the wise Galileo
    Denial of all the great truths he believed, —

Before the whole world to give up his convictions,
    Because the great church said the world had not moved;
Then to swear, before God, that his science was idle,
    And truth was unknown to the facts he had proved.

So, loosing his shackles, they bade the sage listen
    To words from the mouth of the vicar of God:
"Recant thy vile doctrines, and life we will give thee:
    Adhere, and thy road to the grave is soon trod!"

His doctrines — the truth, as proud Rome has acknowledged —
    On low, bended knee, in that vault he renounced;
Yet with joy in their eyes, the high-priests retiring,
    "Confinement for life," as his sentence pronounced.

But as they left him, their malice rekindled
    Fires that their threats had subdued in his breast:
Clanking his chains, with fierce ardor he muttered,
    "But it *does* move, and tyrants can ne'er make it rest."

Belshazzar.

HE midnight hour was drawing on;
　　Flushed in repose lay Babylon;
　　But in the palace of the king
　　　The herd of courtiers shout and sing.
There, in his royal banquet hall,
Belshazzar holds high festival.

The servants sit in glittering rows,
The beakers are drained, the red wine flows;
The beakers clash and the servants sing. —
A pleasing sound to the moody king.
The king's cheeks flush and his wild eyes shine,
His spirit waxes bold with wine,
Until, by maddening passion stung,
He scoffs at God with impious tongue;
And his proud heart swells as he wildly raves,
'Mid shouts of applause from his fawning slaves.
He spoke the word, and his eyes flashed flame!
The ready servants went and came;
Vessels of massive gold they bore,
Of Jehovah's temple the plundered store.

Then seizing a consecrated cup,
The king in his fury fills it up;
He fills, and hastily drains it dry;
From his foaming lips leaps forth the cry,

"Jehovah, at Thee my scorn I fling!
I am Belshazzar, Babylon's king."
Yet scarce had the impious words been said,
When the king's heart shrank with secret dread;
Suddenly died the shout and yell,
A deathlike hush on the tumult fell.

And see! and see! on the white wall high
The form of a hand went slowly by,
And wrote — and wrote in sight of all
Letters of fire upon the wall!
The king sat still, with a stony look,
His trembling knees with terror shook;
The menial throng nor spoke nor stirred;
Fear froze the blood, — no sound was heard.

The magicians came, but none of all
Could read the writing on the wall.
At length to solve those words of flame,
Fearless, but meek, the prophet came.
One glance he gave, and all was clear.
"King! there is reason in thy fear.
Those words proclaim, thy empire ends,
The day of woe and wrath impends.
Weighed in the balance, wanting found,
Thou and thy empire strike the ground!"

That night, by the servants of his train,
Belshazzar, the mighty king, was slain!

LIBERTY.

WITH what pride I used
To walk these hills, and look up to my God,
And bless him that it was so! I loved
Its very storms. I have sat
In my boat at night when, midway o'er the lake,
The stars went out, and down the mountain gorge
The wind came roaring. I have sat and eyed
The thunder breaking from his cloud, and smiled
To see him shake his lightnings o'er my head,
And think I had no master save his own.
You know the jutting cliff round which a track
Up hither winds, whose base is but the brow
To such another one, with scanty room
For two abreast to pass? O'ertaken there
By the mountain blast, I've laid me flat along,
And while gust followed gust more furiously,
As if to sweep me o'er the horrid brink,
And I have thought of other lands, whose storms
Are summer flaws to those of mine, and just
Have wished me there — the thought that mine was free
Has checked that wish; and I have raised my head,
And cried in thraldom to that furious wind,
Blow on! This is the land of liberty!

The Fishermen.

URRAH! the seaward breezes
    Sweep down the bay amain.
Heave up, my lads, the anchor!
    Run up the sail again!
Leave to the lubber landsmen
    The rail-car and the steed;
The stars of heaven shall guide us,
    The breath of heaven shall speed.

From the hill-top looks the steeple,
    And the lighthouse from the sand;
And the scattered pines are waving
    Their farewell from the land.
One glance, my lads, behind us,
    For the homes we leave one sigh,
Ere we take the change and chances
    Of the ocean and the sky.

Now, brothers, for the icebergs
    Of frozen Labrador,
Floating spectral in the moonshine,
    Along the low, black shore!
Where like snow the gannet's feathers
    On Brador's rocks are shed,
And the noisy murr are flying,
    Like black scuds, overhead;

Where in mist the rock is hiding,
  And the sharp reef lurks below,
And the white squall smites in summer,
  And the autumn tempests blow;
Where, through gray and rolling vapor,
  From evening unto morn,
A thousand boats are hailing,
  Horn answering unto horn.

Hurrah for the Red Island,
  With the white cross on its crown!
Hurrah for Meccatina,
  And its mountains bare and brown!
Where the caribou's tall antlers
  O'er the dwarf-wood freely toss,
And the footstep of the mickmack
  Has no sound upon the moss.

There we'll drop our lines, and gather
  Old Ocean's treasures in,
Where'er the mottled mackerel
  Turns up a steel-dark fin.
The sea's our field of harvest,
  Its scaly tribes our grain;
We'll reap the teeming waters
  As at home they reap the plain!

Our wet hands spread the carpet,
  And light the hearth of home;
From our fish, as in the old time,
  The silver coin shall come.

As the demon fled the chamber
　　Where the fish of Tobit lay,
So ours from all our dwellings
　　Shall frighten Want away.

Though the mist upon our jackets
　　In the bitter air congeals,
And our lines wind stiff and slowly
　　From off the frozen reels,
Though the fog be dark around us,
　　And the storm blow high and loud,
We will whistle down the wild wind,
　　And laugh beneath the cloud!

In the darkness as in daylight,
　　On the water as on land,
God's eye is looking on us,
　　And beneath us is his hand!
Death will find us soon or later,
　　On the deck or in the cot;
And we cannot meet him better
　　Than in working out our lot.

Hurrah! hurrah! The west wind
　　Comes freshening down the bay,
The rising sails are filling,—
　　Give way, my lads, give way!
Leave the coward landsman clinging
　　To the dull earth, like a weed.
The stars of heaven shall guide us,
　　The breath of heaven shall speed!

Excelsior.

THE shades of night were falling fast,
As through an Alpine village passed
A youth, who bore, 'mid snow and ice,
A banner, with the strange device,
    Excelsior!

His brow was sad; his eye, beneath,
Flashed like a falchion from its sheath;
And like a silver clarion rung
The accents of that unknown tongue,
    Excelsior!

In happy homes he saw the light
Of household fires gleam warm and bright.
Above, the spectral glaciers shone;
And from his lips escaped a groan,
    Excelsior!

"Try not the pass!" the old man said;
"Dark lowers the tempest overhead!
The roaring torrent is deep and wide!"
And loud that clarion voice replied,
    Excelsior!

"Oh! stay," the maiden said, "and rest
Thy weary head upon this breast!"
A tear stood in his bright blue eye;
But still he answered, with a sigh,
    Excelsior!

"Beware the pine-tree's withered branch!
Beware the awful avalanche!"
This was the peasant's last good-night.
A voice replied, far up the height,
    Excelsior!

At break of day, as heavenward
The pious monks of St. Bernard
Uttered the oft-repeated prayer,
A voice cried, through the startled air,
    Excelsior!

A traveller by the faithful hound,
Half buried in the snow, was found,
Still grasping in his hand of ice
The banner with the strange device,
    Excelsior!

There, in the twilight cold and gray,
Lifeless, but beautiful, he lay;
And from the sky, serene and far,
A voice fell, like a falling star,—
    Excelsior!

The Soldier.

OR gold the merchant ploughs the main,
  The farmer ploughs the manor;
But glory is the soldier's prize,
  The soldier's wealth is honor.
The brave poor soldier ne'er despise;
  Nor count him as a stranger;
Remember, he's his country's stay
  In day and hour o' danger.

John Maynard.

'TWAS on Lake Erie's broad expanse,
   One bright midsummer day,
The gallant steamer, Ocean Queen,
   Swept proudly on her way.
Bright faces clustered on the deck,
   Or, leaning o'er the side,
Watched carelessly the feathery foam
   That flecked the rippling tide.

A seaman sought the captain's side,
   A moment whispered low:
The captain's swarthy face grew pale;
   He hurried down below.
Alas, too late! Though quick and sharp
   And clear his orders came,
No human efforts could avail
   To quench th' insidious flame.

The bad news quickly reached the deck,
   It sped from lip to lip,
And ghastly faces everywhere
   Looked from the doomèd ship.
"Is there no hope, no chance of life?"
   A hundred lips implore.
"But one," the captain made reply;
   "To run the ship on shore."

A sailor whose heroic soul
  That hour should yet reveal,
By name John Maynard, Eastern born,
  Stood calmly at the wheel.
"Head her southeast!" the captain shouts,
  Above the smothered roar, —
"Head her southeast without delay!
  Make for the nearest shore!"

John Maynard watched the nearing flames,
  But still, with steady hand,
He grasped the wheel, and steadfastly
  He steered the ship to land.
"John Maynard, can you still hold out?"
  He heard the captain cry.
A voice from out the stifling smoke
  Faintly responds, "Ay, ay!"

But half a mile! A hundred hands
  Stretch eagerly to shore.
But half a mile! That distance sped,
  Peril shall all be o'er.
But half a mile! Yet stay! The flames
  No longer slowly creep,
But gather round the helmsman bold
  With fierce, impetuous sweep.

"John Maynard," with an anxious voice,
  The captain cries once more,
"Stand by the wheel five minutes yet,
  And we will reach the shore."

Through flames and smoke that dauntless heart
  Responded firmly still,
Unawed, though face to face with death,
  "With God's good help, I will!"

The flames approach with giant strides,
  They scorch his hands and brow;
One arm disabled seeks his side:
  Ah, he is conquered now!
But no; his teeth are firmly set,
  He crushes down his pain;
His knee upon the stanchion pressed,
  He guides the ship again.

One moment yet, one moment yet!
  Brave heart, thy task is o'er!
The pebbles grate beneath the keel,
  The steamer touches shore.
Three hundred grateful voices rise
  In praise to God, that He
Hath saved them from the fearful fire
  And from th' ingulfing sea.

But where is he, that helmsman bold?
  The captain saw him reel;
His nerveless hands released their task,
  He sank beside the wheel.
The wave received his lifeless corpse,
  Blackened with smoke and fire.
God rest him! Never hero had
  A nobler funeral pyre.

Excalibur.

THEN spake King Arthur to Sir Bedivere:
"The sequel of to-day unsolders all
The goodliest fellowship of famous knights
Whereof this world holds record. Such a sleep
They sleep, — the men I loved. I think that we
Shall never more, at any future time,
Delight our souls with talk of knightly deeds,
Walking about the gardens and the halls
Of Camelot, as in the days that were.
I perish by this people which I made, —
Though Merlin swear that I should come again
To rule once more; but let what will be, be:
I am so deeply smitten through the helm
That without help I cannot last till morn.
Thou therefore take my brand Excalibur,
Which was my pride: for thou rememberest how
In those old days, one summer noon, an arm
Rose up from out the bosom of the lake,
Clothed in white samite, mystic, wonderful,
Holding the sword; and how I rowed across
And took it, and have worn it, like a king:
And, wheresoever I am sung or told

In after-time, this also shall be known:
But now delay not: take Excalibur,
And fling him far into the middle mere.
Watch what thou seest, and lightly bring me word."

    .   .   .

Then quickly rose Sir Bedivere, and ran,
And, leaping down the ridges lightly, plunged
Among the bulrush beds, and clutched the sword,
And strongly wheeled and threw it. The great brand
Made lightnings in the splendor of the moon,
And flashing round and round, and whirled in an arch,
Shot like a streamer of the northern morn,
Seen where the moving isles of winter shock
By night, with noises of the northern sea.
So flashed and fell the brand Excalibur:
But ere he dipt the surface, rose an arm
Clothed in white samite, mystic, wonderful,
And caught him by the hilt, and brandished him
Three times, and drew him under in the mere.
And lightly went the other to the king.

The Death of Arthur.

THEN saw they how there hove a dusky barge,
Dark as a funeral scarf from stem to stern,
Beneath them; and descending they were ware
That all the decks were dense with stately forms
Black-stoled, black-hooded, like a dream; by these
Three Queens with crowns of gold, and from them rose
A cry that shivered to the tingling stars,
And, as it were one voice, an agony
Of lamentation, like a wind that shrills
All night in a waste land, where no one comes,
Or hath come since the making of the world.

Then murmured Arthur, "Place me in the barge."
So to the barge they came. There those three Queens
Put forth their hands, and took the king, and wept.
  .   .   .   .   .

And slowly answered Arthur from the barge:
"The old order changeth, yielding place to new,
And God fulfils himself in many ways,
Lest one good custom should corrupt the world.
Comfort thyself: what comfort is in me?
I have lived my life, and that which I have done
May He within himself make pure! but thou,

If thou shouldst never see my face again,
Pray for my soul. More things are wrought by prayer
Than this world dreams of. Wherefore, let thy voice
Rise like a fountain for me night and day.
For what are men better than sheep or goats
That nourish a blind life within the brain,
If, knowing God, they lift not hands of prayer
Both for themselves and those who call them friend?
For so the whole round earth is every way
Bound by gold chains about the feet of God.
But now farewell. I am going a long way
With these thou seest — if indeed I go —
(For all my mind is clouded with a doubt)
To the island-valley of Avilion,
Where falls not hail, or rain, or any snow,
Nor ever wind blows loudly; but it lies
Deep-meadowed, happy, fair with orchard-lawns
And bowery hollows crowned with summer sea,
Where I will heal me of my grievous wound."

So said he, and the barge with oar and sail
Moved from the brink, like some full-breasted swan
That, fluting a wild carol ere her death,
Ruffles her pure cold plume, and takes the flood
With swarthy webs.

A Wet Sheet and a Flowing Sea.

A WET sheet and a flowing sea,
  A wind that follows fast,
And fills the white and rustling sail,
  And bends the gallant mast.
And bends the gallant mast, my boys,
  While, like the eagle free,
Away the good ship flies, and leaves
  Old England on the lee.

O, for a soft and gentle wind!
  I heard a fair one cry;
But give to me the swelling breeze,
  And white waves heaving high.
The white waves heaving high, my lads,
  The good ship tight and free, —
The world of waters is our home,
  And merry men are we.

THE LEAP OF CURTIUS.

WITHIN Rome's forum, suddenly, a wide gap opened in a night,
Astounding those who gazed on it,—a strange, terrific sight.
In Senate all their sages met, and, seated in their chairs of state,
Their faces blanched with deadly fear, debated long and late.

A sign inimical to Rome, they deemed it,—a prognostic dire,
A visitation from the gods, in token of their ire.
Yet how to have their minds resolved, how ascertain in this their need,
Beyond the shadow of a doubt, if thus it were indeed?

In silence brooded they awhile, unbroken by a single word,
While from the capital without the lightest sounds were heard.
Then rose the eldest magistrate, a tall old man, with locks like snow,
Straight as a dart, and with an eye that oft had quelled the foe.

And thus, with ripe, sonorous voice, no note or tone of which did shake,
Or indicate the wear of time, the aged Nestor spake:
"Fathers, the Oracle is nigh: to it then let us promptly send,
And at the shrine inquire what this dread marvel doth portend.

"And if to Rome it augurs ill, then ask we, ere it be too late,
How we may best avert the doom, and save the sacred state,—
That state to every Roman dear, as dear as brother, friend, or wife,
For which each true-born son would give, if needful, even life.

"For what, O fathers! what were life apart from altar, hearth, and home?
Yea, is not all our highest good bound up with that of Rome?
And now adjourn we for a space, till three full days have circled round,
And on the morning of the fourth, let each one here be found."

Then gat they up, and gloomily for such short interval did part,
For they were Romans stanch and tried, and sad was every heart.
The fourth day dawned, and when they met, the Oracle's response was
    known:
Something most precious in the chasm to close it must be thrown.

But if *unclosed* it shall remain, thereon shall follow Rome's decay,
And all the splendor of her state shall pale and pass away.
Something most precious! What the gift that may prevent the pending fate,
What costly offering will the gods indeed propitiate?

While this they pondered, lo! a sound of footsteps fell on every ear,
And in their midst a Roman youth did presently appear.
Apollo's brow, a mien like Mars, in Beauty's mould he seemed new-made,
As on his golden hair the sun with dazzling dalliance played.

'T is Marcus Curtius! Purer blood none there could boast, and none
    more brave:
There stands the youthful patriot, come, a Roman, Rome to save.
His own young life, he offers that, yea, volunteers *himself* to throw
Within the cleft to make it close, and stay the heavy woe.

And now on horseback, fully armed, behold him, for the hour hath come.
The Roman guards keep watch and ward, and beats the muffled drum.
The consuls, proctors, soothsayers, within the forum group around,
Young Curtius in the saddle sits, — there yawns the severed ground.

Each pulse is stayed. He lifts his helm, and bares his forehead to the sky,
And to the broad, blue heaven above upturns his flashing eye.
"O Rome, O country best beloved, thou land in which I first drew breath,
I render back the life thou gav'st, to rescue *thee* from death!"

Then spurring on his gallant steed, a last and brief farewell he said,
And leapt within the gaping gulf, *which closed above his head.*

The Ride from Ghent to Aix.

I SPRANG to the stirrup, and Joris, and he;
I galloped, Dirck galloped, we galloped all three.
"Good speed!" cried the watch, as the gate-bolts undrew;
"Speed!" echoed the wall to us galloping through.
Behind shut the postern, the lights sank to rest,
And into the midnight we galloped abreast.

Not a word to each other; we kept the great pace
Neck by neck, stride for stride, never changing our place.
I turned in my saddle and made its girths tight,
Then shortened each stirrup, and set the pique right,
Rebuckled the cheek-strap, chained slacker the bit,
Nor galloped less steadily Roland a whit.

'Twas moonset at starting; but while we drew near
Lokeren, the cocks crew and twilight dawned clear;
At Boom, a great yellow star came out to see;
At Düffield, 'twas morning, as plain as could be;
And from Mecheln church-steeple we heard the half-chime,
So Joris broke the silence with, "Yet there is time!"

At Aerschot, up leaped of a sudden the sun,
And against him the cattle stood black every one.

To stare through the mist at us galloping past,
And I saw my stout galloper Roland, at last,
With resolute shoulders, each butting away
The haze, as some bluff river headland its spray.

And his low head and crest, just one sharp ear bent back
For my voice, and the other pricked out on his track;
And one eye's black intelligence, ever that glance
O'er its white edge at me, his own master, askance;
And the thick, heavy spume-flakes which aye and anon
His fierce lips shook upwards on galloping on.

By Hasselt, Dirck groaned; and cried Joris, "Stay spur!
Your Roos galloped bravely, the fault 's not in her.
We 'll remember at Aix!"—for one heard the quick wheeze
Of her chest, saw the stretched neck and staggering knees,
And sunk tail, and horrible heave of the flank,
As down on her haunches she shuddered and sank.

So we were left galloping, Joris and I,
Past Looz and past Tongrés, no cloud in the sky;
The broad sun above laughed a pitiless laugh,
'Neath our feet broke the brittle, bright stubble like chaff,
Till over by Dalhem a dome-spire sprang white,
And, "Gallop," gasped Joris, "for Aix is in sight!

"How they 'll greet us!" And all in a moment his roan
Rolled neck and croup over, lay dead as a stone;
And there was my Roland to bear the whole weight
Of the news which alone could save Aix from her fate,
With his nostrils like pits full of blood to the brim
And with circles of red for his eye-sockets' rim.

Then I cast loose my buffcoat, each hoister let fall,
Shook off both my jack-boots, let go belt and all,
Stood up in the stirrup, leaned, patted his ear,
Called my Roland his pet name, my horse without peer;
Clapped my hands, laughed and sang,—any noise, bad or good,
Till at length into Aix Roland galloped and stood.

And all I remember is friends flocking around
As I sat with his head 'twixt my knees on the ground,
And no voice but was praising this Roland of mine,
As I poured down his throat our last measure of wine,
Which (the burgesses voted by common consent)
Was no more than his due who brought good news from Ghent.

A YARN.

"'T IS Saturday night, and our watch below.
What heed we, boys, how the breezes blow,
While our cans are brimmed with the sparkling flow?
Come, Jack, uncoil, as we pass the grog,
And spin us a yarn from memory's log."

Jack's brawny chest like the broad sea heaved,
While his loving lip to the beaker cleaved;
And he drew his tarred and well-saved sleeve
Across his mouth, as he drained the can,
And thus to his listening mates began: —

"When I sailed, a boy, in the schooner Mike,
No bigger, I trow, than a marlinespike —
But I've told ye the tale ere now, belike?"
"Go on!" each voice re-echoed,
And the tar thrice hemmed, and thus he said: —

"A stanch-built craft as the waves e'er bore —
We had loosed our sail for home once more,
Freighted full deep from Labrador,
When a cloud one night rose on our lee,
That the heart of the stoutest quailed to see.

"And voices wild with the winds were blent,
As our bark her prow to the waters bent;
And the seamen muttered their discontent —
Muttered and nodded ominously —
But the mate, right carelessly whistled he.

"'Our bark may never outride the gale.
'T is a pitiless night! The pattering hail
Hath coated each spar as 't were in mail;
And our sails are riven before the breeze,
While our cordage and shrouds into icicles freeze!'

"Thus spake the skipper beside the mast,
While the arrowy sleet fell thick and fast;
And our bark drove onward before the blast
That goaded the waves, till the angry main
Rose up and strove with the hurricane.

"Up spake the mate, and his tone was gay, —
'Shall we at this hour to fear give way?
We must labor, in sooth, as well as pray.
Out, shipmates, and grapple home yonder sail,
That flutters in ribbons before the gale!'

"Loud swelled the tempest, and rose the shriek,
'Save, save! we are sinking! A leak! a leak!'
And the hale old skipper's tawny cheek
Was cold, as 't were sculptured in marble there,
And white as the foam or his own white hair.

"The wind piped shrilly, the wind piped loud,
It shrieked 'mong the cordage, it howled in the shroud,
And the sleet fell thick from the cold, dun cloud;
But high over all, in tones of glee,
The voice of the mate rang cheerily, —

"Now, men, for your wives' and your sweethearts' sakes!
Cheer, messmates, cheer! Quick! man the brakes!
We'll gain on the leak ere the skipper wakes;
And though our peril your hearts appall,
Ere dawns the morrow we'll laugh at the squall.'

"He railed at the tempest, he laughed at its threats,
He played with his fingers like castanets;
Yet think not that he, in his mirth, forgets
That the plank he is riding this hour at sea
May launch him the next to eternity!

"The white-haired skipper turned away,
And lifted his hands, as it were to pray;
But his look spoke plainly as look could say,
The boastful thought of the Pharisee, —
'Thank God, I'm not hardened as others be!'

"But the morning dawned, and the waves sank low,
And the winds, o'erwearied, forebore to blow;
And our bark lay there in the golden glow, —
Flashing she lay in the bright sunshine,
An ice-sheathed hulk on the cold, still brine.

"Well, shipmates, my yarn is almost spun —
The cold and the tempest their work had done,
And I was the last, lone, living one,
Clinging, benumbed, to that wave-girt wreck,
While the dead around me bestrewed the deck.

"Yea, the dead were round me everywhere!
The skipper gray, in the sunlight there,
Still lifted his paralyzed hands in prayer;
And the mate, whose tones through the darkness leapt,
In the silent hush of the morning slept.

"Oh, bravely he perished who sought to save
Our storm-tossed bark from the pitiless wave,
And her crew from a yawning and fathomless grave,
Crying, 'Messmates, cheer!' with a bright, glad smile,
And praying, 'Be merciful, God!' the while.

"True to his trust, to his last chill gasp,
The helm lay clutched in his stiff, cold grasp:
You might scarcely in death undo the clasp;
And his crisp, brown locks were dank and thin,
And the icicles hung from his bearded chin.

"My timbers have weathered, since, many a gale;
And when life's tempests this hulk assail,
And the binnacle-lamp in my breast burns pale,
'Cheer, messmates, cheer!' to my heart I say,
'We must labor, in sooth, as well as pray.'"

www.ingramcontent.com/pod-product-compliance
Lightning Source LLC
Chambersburg PA
CBHW030243170426
43202CB00009B/602